The Race Of A
LIFETIME:
Second Wind

Michael Layne

A True Story about Spiritual Growth, Grace,
Mercy, Faith, Endurance & Being Anchored in
the Foundation of Christ's Love.

authorHOUSE®

AuthorHouse™
1663 Liberty Drive
Bloomington, IN 47403
www.authorhouse.com
Phone: 1 (800) 839-8640

Published by AuthorHouse 07/27/2016

ISBN: 978-1-5246-1996-1 (sc)
ISBN: 978-1-5246-1995-4 (e)

Library of Congress Control Number: 2016911860

Print information available on the last page.

NASB

This book is dedicated to my lovely wife and amazing daughter. You mean the world to me. I thank God for both of you. You both keep me on my toes. I pray that I will continue to lead you as God intended me to from the beginning.

This book is dedicated to the matriarch of our family, Maybelle Jamison, whose light continues to shine for Christ no matter what the circumstance may be. Granny, you are a powerful example of how we should love the Lord with everything we have and love each other the way Christ commanded us to. May your love continue to spread from generation to generation.

This book is dedicated to my brothers and sisters— The Six!— and the rest of my family, both near and far.

This book is dedicated to all of the friends who've supported me in my walk with Christ.

May we all continue to seek, to follow, and to obey the teachings of Jesus Christ.

Rest In Peace Uncle Alfonso.

THE TRUTH

Jesus died on the cross for the sins of mankind. Those who believe in the birth, the death, and the resurrection of Jesus Christ will be saved for eternity. We are saved by grace through faith in Jesus Christ! This truth, which we call the Gospel, must reach everyone.

Contents

The Truth vii

1. Planting, Watering, & Spiritual Growth 1

2. My Second Wind..2

3. Engaged and Still Learning: Placed in
    God's Position 4

4. Wedding Theme: An Answered Prayer 7

5. Follow the Leader..20

6. My First Experience at Sheepfold Church 22

7. First Steps: A Servant Gets in the Game 24

8. The Gift of Faith: A Spiritual Gift Is
    Given to Me 26

9. A Pause for Reflection 28

10. Back to Panama...29

11. Submerged in Him: Baptism, October 4, 2009 ...38

12. It Was Time To Meet Faith Evans 40

13. I Accepted the Call: God Put Something
    Inside Me..52

14. My First Sermon and a Special Gift 54

15. A Journey Home 61

16. A Season Is Over: My Sheepfold Church
    Departure 97

17. A Child Is Born: A Gift from the Lord............99

18. "Where Is Your Faith?"................................. 103

19. Falling Short in God's Eyes: My
    Confession of Devotion.................................. 108

20. How the Trayvon Martin Tragedy
    Touched My Life 111
21. A Quick Pause: A Moment in His Word 119
22. Making It Personal: "How Are Your
    Brothers and Sisters?" "How Is Your Mom?" ... 121
23. The Journey Continues: I'm Still on
    Assignment and Not Turning Back 125
Acknowledgments 127
About the Author 131

1

PLANTING, WATERING, & SPIRITUAL GROWTH

Paul says in 1 Corinthians 3:6–7, "I planted, Apollos watered, but God was causing the growth. So then neither the one who plants nor the one who waters is anything, but God who causes the growth." I have found this passage of Scripture to be true because seeds of the Gospel were planted in me early on in life. God then brought Ericka (eventually my wife) into my life to water those seeds.

Now that my eyes are fully open, I can see the full truth of the Gospel. God is in charge of my spiritual growth. I am well into my journey of learning from and growing in Him.

2

MY SECOND WIND

The Race of a Lifetime is a true story about spiritual growth, grace, mercy, faith, endurance, and being anchored to the foundation of Christ's love. When writing this book, I often thought of the words sung by Kim McFarland in the song "For the Good of Them." She sings,

> The race is not given to the swift nor to the strong but to the one that endureth, until the end.
> There will be problems and sometimes you walk alone but I know, that I know, that I know ... things will work out, yes they will
> For good of them ... who love the Lord.

These are awesome words of encouragement. They are like a second wind that is needed when you're running the longest race called *life*. You need that extra push to keep running and enduring as you follow Christ. We have a hope in Romans 8:28 that says, "And we know that God causes all things to work together for good to those who love God, to those who are called according to His purpose."

Will there be obstacles? Yes! Will there be doubt? Yes! Will you fall at times? Yes! Will there be times of weakness? Yes! However, Christ tells us to keep going because He's the Author and the Finisher of our faith. No matter what trial we face each day, we are being conformed to the image of Jesus Christ. We must press on in faith. I'm going to keep running for Him because my Lord, Savior, and God is omnipotent! He has all power, so I'm in good hands.

3

ENGAGED AND STILL LEARNING

Placed in God's Position

I was on my knees asking for Ericka's hand in marriage at the exact place she had prayed and had asked God for a husband. Behind the scenes, God was at work. God was setting something up for His glory by putting two people together whom He knew would glorify Him. God ordained that moment.

He had directed my path to Texas for many reasons. I was about to start a new journey. Of course, with any journey, there would be more work to do and things to learn as I continued to move forward. Most of all, there was no turning back to the things I had done in the Midwest.

Now that I was a new creature in Christ, my life would constantly be changing. As always, He knew where I needed to be. I was in His will and headed in the right direction.

The Next Steps

After I got the famous, "Yes," from Ericka, our next step was to plan our wedding. I had no clue where or how to do this, but Ericka was the expert. It must have been an innate thing for her. She knew how to get the ball rolling.

The list of things to do before our wedding grew. We had to think about our engagement pictures, wedding venues, engagement party, marriage counseling sessions, save-the-date invitations, honeymoon, and securing a pastor to officiate our wedding. The list of things to do was long and expensive, but we both kept moving forward. We knew God had placed us together for His purpose. As we moved toward our wedding, God would teach us many lessons that we would need for our marriage.

So You Wanna Get Married?

Someone strongly suggested that we should go through marriage counseling before our wedding day. I remember thinking, *Hey, I love this woman, and she loves me, so why do we need marriage counseling? We have things covered.* I didn't know I was in for a rude awakening. Ericka and I thought we knew each other so well, but after our thirteen-week counseling sessions, we realized there were things we needed to work on before and during our marriage. We planned to spend the rest of our lives together but did not fully grasp the concept, "Until death do us part."

I would be the head of our household and would have to learn how to love Ericka as Christ loved the church. I had no clue what that meant, especially in the beginning of my walk with Christ. Honestly, I still haven't grasped this command. According to Ephesians 5:25–27, Christ loved the church even when she was dirty. In other words, Christ demonstrated His love by dying for imperfect people. I knew I had to demonstrate this same love toward Ericka and I had some learning to do to demonstrate this same love as a future husband.

In the learning process, I asked, "Do I have to love and lead Ericka back to God?" God let me know how serious He took marriage. Marriage was not a game. I hadn't known that when I made a commitment to Ericka, I had also made a commitment to God.

As always, I had so much to learn. God would not allow me to turn my back on the vision He had given to me to marry Ericka. Ericka was the wife He had designed just for me. We were getting ready to make it official before family, friends, and most importantly, the Lord.

4

WEDDING THEME

An Answered Prayer

We had jumped over every hurdle when our big day finally arrived on July 26, 2008. I could not believe Ericka and I were getting married. Everything was planned. Everything was in place. It amazed me that both sides of our families would be there to witness and to help us celebrate our union. Our wedding theme was called, "An Answered Prayer," because God had answered Ericka's prayer for a husband, and that person was me!

On top of Ericka's answered prayer, God blessed me by making Ericka my wife. God gave me a great woman. I would soon understand Proverbs 18:22, which says, "He who finds a wife finds a good thing and obtains favor from the lord" (NASB).

Favor from God was unexplainable. Favor from God was something I did not deserve, yet He gave to me my whole life. God was uniting me with a woman who was going to be my helper, and our marriage would be for the purpose of glorifying Him. I could not believe it!

Things were happening at a rapid pace. At the right time, God used Ericka to teach me about the Gospel, which is the good news about Jesus Christ. Soon, He would call me to lead and teach her as her future husband. Through all of this, my passion to learn more about Jesus Christ continued to grow.

Why did God love me so much? I would gradually learn the reason during the course of my journey. As always, God was with me every step of the way and showed me what I needed to know in His time.

At the Altar

Ericka and I stood at the altar in the Green Oaks Wedding Chapel. We were blessed and had so much to be thankful for because many loved ones were there to witness our day.

My best friends, Ed from Indiana and Tone from Minnesota, had come to be with me. Ed and Tone had been influential in my life. Now they were my best men. My good friend Harold was my groomsman, so I had three strong men supporting me.

On a special note, I even had family members who had come from as far as Illinois, New York, and Massachusetts to celebrate our union. Ericka's family had come from Texas and Louisiana. It was amazing to see everyone there.

I was even more honored that my childhood coach, Coach Gardner, would be our officiating pastor. He had traveled from Indiana to be with us.

Everything was ready. Many witnesses were with us, and most of all, God was in the chapel. A new family and covenant would be united in God.

As I stood there at the altar waiting for my bride, my heart continued to race. Again, I could not believe I was getting married. My life was changing right before my very eyes. I hadn't seen this day coming when I had moved from Minnesota to Texas. Ed a pastor, my best friend and one of my best men had been correct when he had prophesied, just two years prior to this day, that I would meet my wife in Texas. Now I was at the altar and was ready to receive my bride.

The Ceremony

As Ericka and I stood at the altar and faced each other, Pastor Gardner explained that God had originally ordained marriage between Adam and Eve. God told Adam in Genesis 2:18, "It is not good for the man to be alone; I will make him a helper suitable for him" (NASB).

As I would soon learn, Ericka was my helper. As always, God knew who and what I needed in my life. He knew I needed a woman who was grounded in her faith in Christ and who would inspire me to grow in my faith.

The journey of following Christ, as I later found out, would not be easy. However, I learned that the Lord would always be with me during that journey. I understood what David felt in Psalm 23. The Lord was indeed my Shepherd too.

After Pastor Gardner gave us a history lesson on marriage and becoming one flesh, it was time to make our commitment official in the eyes of God. Pastor Gardner said,

> Michael Layne, will you have this woman to be your wedded wife, to live together after God's ordinance in the holy estate of matrimony, will you love her, comfort her, honor her, and keep her in sickness and in health, and forsaking all others, keep yourself only unto her so long as you both shall live, you will answer I will.

I answered, "I will." Then Pastor Gardner turned to Ericka and gave her the same divine charge. Ericka in turn answered, "I will."

As Ericka and I faced each other and held each other's hands, we said our wedding vows. Pastor Gardner told me to repeat after him, "I, Michael Layne, take thee Ericka ... " I accidentally combined the first part of my fiancé's middle name with her first name. The audience let out an, "Aw," that reminded me of the sound a crowd makes when someone misses a critical three-point shot or fails to clear a specific height in the pole vault or high jump events. I simply could not get Ericka's full name out of my mouth fast enough. When I finally did, I butchered her name as she continued to hold my hand and say, "It's okay!" She knew I was nervous but smiled back at me.

After I said my vows, it was Ericka's turn. As Ericka said her vows to me, Pastor Gardner told her to repeat my name after him. For a split second, my heart stopped. As the audience was on the edge of their seats, Ericka said, "I, Ericka, take thee, Mmmmm ... " I thought Ericka had forgotten my name. Then she said, "I'm just playing'." The audience erupted in laughter as she jokingly let everyone know that she was kidding. This event lit up the chapel.

Ericka laughed until she saw Pastor Gardner's face. He had been laughing too but now had a serious look on his face, as if to let Ericka know, he had a wedding to officiate. It was back to business for him. Ericka quickly regained her composure and told Pastor Gardner she was ready to say her vows.

After Ericka said her vows to me, Pastor Gardner immediately stated "Then each belongs to the other, for richer or poorer, for better or worse, in sickness or in health till death alone shall part you."

After these words of confirmation, Pastor Gardner went on to discuss the history and significance of the wedding ring. He told us that the ring had always been used to seal important covenants. He called it a golden circle. When he said this, it took me back to the track where I first proposed to Ericka. I thought about the circle being united and the significance of the ring. Our marriage was sealed in an unbreakable circle. The pure gold symbolized our love for each other. It would be pure and would grow brighter and brighter as time went by. Ericka and I placed the rings on each other's fingers. As we did, I realized there were still some things that we needed to do to make our wedding official in the site of God.

Our First Family Communion

Now that Ericka and I had been united as one, we would take communion together for the first time as a family. Ericka and I strongly believed the most important foundation in our marriage was God's greatest gift, His Son, Jesus Christ. Partaking in communion was very important in our Christian faith because it symbolized all that Christ did to save a dying world from sin. We did this to remember that Christ suffered and died for our sins. It's through the shedding of His blood and His death that makes those of us who believe right with God.

While Ericka and I stood at the table where we would light our unity candle and take communion, Pastor Gardner would soon officiate our first communion together. Once we lit our unity candle, we prepared for communion.

Pastor Gardner then boldly said, "And Jesus took the bread and blessed it and broke it and gave it unto them and said take ye eat this is My body." Ericka and I ate the bread, which symbolized the broken body of Christ. Pastor Gardner went on to say, "And He took the cup and He gave it unto them and said take ye and drink ye all of this, for this is the new testament in My blood." Ericka and I then drank our cups of juice, which symbolized the blood of Christ that was shed for our sins. Pastor Gardner continued,

And afterwards, they sang a hymn and went out into the Mount of Olives, they did not know that Jesus would soon be taken prisoner and that they would be afraid to show their faces. We like the disciples don't know what fears tomorrow hold but unlike them we have the knowledge that on the third day morning, Jesus rose from the grave with all power in His hand. It is that knowledge that will sustain you in the days to come.

God was speaking through Pastor Gardner with a voice like thunder as he shared the Gospel with everyone in the chapel. It was an experience to hear him speak and this was a powerful moment in our ceremony. Our marriage was officially sealed.

Officially United

After we took communion, Pastor Gardner closed our wedding ceremony with these words,

Having pledged your faith in and love to each other in the site of God and these assembled witnesses and having sealed your solemn vows by giving and receiving the rings, acting with the authority vested in me as a minister of the Gospel by the state of Indiana and looking to heaven for divine sanction, I pronounce you husband and wife. What God has joined together, let no man put asunder. You may salute your bride.

I gave my wife a soft, warm kiss. It was official. Ericka and I were married. We were now Mr. and Mrs. Michael Layne. Our family and friends clapped and cheered loudly.

Jumping the Broom

Before Ericka and I started the festivities of our wedding night, we had a special African tradition that our ancestors had performed many years ago. We would jump the broom. The jumping of the broom symbolized sweeping away our former, single lives, problems, and concerns and moving into a new adventure as husband and wife. The straw of the broom represented the brushing away of our cares and worries. The strong, wooden handle represented the strength of our commitment to each other.

One, two, three ... Ericka and I jumped over the broom. We were ready to start our journey into holy matrimony. We exited the chapel and entered the reception area. Our wedding venue was designed so that people could walk directly from the chapel into the reception area to eat and dine rather than having to relocate to another facility.

We had planned our wedding for months, but the ceremony only lasted eighteen minutes. Overall, we had a wonderful evening of fellowship with family and friends. Our night consisted of food, laughing, dancing, and many photos. Ericka and I were blessed and thankful for all that took place on our wedding day.

The journey begins with many lessons to
learn. Christ was with us through it all.

Honeymoon: Mexico, Here We Come

Ericka and I planned to spend our honeymoon in Barcelo Maya Beach, Mexico. This would be the first time Ericka left US soil. I felt proud that I was already taking Ericka to places she had never seen before. I could not wait to board the plane and get away after a long weekend of festivities with family and friends. Ericka and I had truly been blessed by all the love and support we had received on our wedding day, but now it was time to be on our own.

Again, I was constantly amazed that I was now married and the leader of the Layne household. I had never seen this day coming. I felt blessed at what God had ordained.

Once we arrived in Mexico, we went to our hotel and checked out the scenery. We had planned to have fun, to eat, and to relax, and that's just what we did. We enjoyed our honeymoon in Mexico.

Michael Layne

5

FOLLOW THE LEADER

Continually Growing in Christ

Paul says in Philippians 1:6, "For I am confident of this very thing, that He who began a good work in you will perfect it until the day of Christ Jesus." When I accepted Jesus Christ as my Lord and Savior in 2007, I did not know I still had a long way to go to develop my faith in Christ. I was a baby in Christ but I would soon experience Christ on a new level. Christ would not leave me as a baby Christian, but my growth in Him would be gradual. Every step I took in Christ would teach me something I needed to know. I had a lot of learning to do.

When I got married, God immediately placed me in charge of leading Ericka back to Him. This would be my first ministry. How in the world was I going to do this? God already had a plan. He told me to leave our mega church in Grand Prairie, Texas (where I had accepted Christ), and to go to a smaller, newer church called Sheepfold Church, located in Fort Worth, Texas.

There was nothing wrong with the mega church I had attended in Grand Prairie, but God knew I needed to be at Sheepfold for spiritual growth and development.

He knew I needed hands-on learning in a smaller setting as I continued to grow spiritually. God guided me to Sheepfold Church because He knew it would gradually help me maximize my life in Christ. Day by day, I would be conformed to the image of His Son, which was God's ultimate mission for those who believed in Jesus Christ.

Sheepfold Church

Before Ericka and I transitioned to Sheepfold Church, we occasionally visited Sheepfold because our close friends continually told us about the great teaching that went on there. Our friends were correct!

Each time I attended Sheepfold Church I learned something new about Christ. I grew slowly as I was spiritually fed. Something was happening inside me.

God's vision is never wrong. He had given me the vision of Sheepfold Church as the place where Ericka and I needed to be. I had to face small challenges before our transition. I had received the vision of leaving the mega church, but Ericka had not. She had dedicated more than eight years of service to the mega church we had been attending in Grand Prairie, so this would not be an easy move for her.

I wondered, *Who am I to take Ericka away from her home church? I'm just a beginner in Christ.* It was through constant prayer and many discussions that Ericka was able to trust God and follow me. It was only a matter of time before we joined Sheepfold Church and made it our new church home.

6

MY FIRST EXPERIENCE AT SHEEPFOLD CHURCH

Pastor West of Sheepfold Church knew God's Word very well and helped me grow in Christ. There were two sermons I would never forget where Pastor West talked about the Christian walk.

In one sermon, he said, "It's one thing to know that you are saved in Christ and that nothing can separate you from the love of God but Satan on the other hand is going to make your life miserable. When anyone has accepted Christ as their Lord and Savior, they have placed a target on their back and Satan wants to take you out."

In another sermon, Pastor West pointed out four things that challenged our love for others. The four things that came against love were

Suffering: How do you love when you're suffering?

Society: Society has a different view of love that goes against God's view of love.

Satan: Satan has no love and wants to kill, steal, and destroy you.

Flesh: Our own sinful nature battles against the Spirit of God.

Pastor West did not know he was helping me in my walk with Christ. When he explained these things to me in greater detail, a burden lifted off my shoulders, and I grew in my faith in Christ.

When I had accepted Jesus Christ as my Lord and Savior, I learned that I had been saved and had been sealed as a child of God forever. However, I still had a lot of growing to do before I would be spiritually mature.

Pastor West taught me so much. He said I would never be perfect in this life but would be made perfect when I was officially with Christ in heaven. He told me the Christian walk was a lifelong process where I would still encounter trials and tribulations and would even make mistakes. Pastor West let me know Satan would be in the background always trying to take me out, but Jesus would be right by my side.

As a constant reminder, Jesus conquered death and defeated Satan when He died on the cross for our sins and rose from the dead. In my walk with Christ, I had to learn to rely on His power alone. I had to let Christ live through me, but it would be a battle and a lifelong journey.

7

FIRST STEPS

A Servant Gets in the Game

> But the greatest among you shall be your servant.
> (Matt. 23:11)

Many of us want to be great or first at something. If you're a competitor, it's in your nature. I know that Jesus is the greatest and is always first, yet He says in Matthew 20:26–28 that whoever wants to become great must be a servant. Whoever wants to be first must serve others like a slave does. Jesus also makes it clear in this passage of Scripture that He has set the example we should follow of being both a slave and a servant. He did not come to be served by others but to serve them. His ultimate goal was to give His life to save people.

When I officially joined Sheepfold Church, I started my next step, which was learning about Christ by being a servant. It was one thing to become a member of a church but another to serve in the church. Ericka already knew how to serve others, but I had to learn to serve as Christ served. Many churches called it, "Get in the game."

24

Pastor West taught me that God gave every believer in Jesus Christ at least one spiritual gift to help the church grow and to glorify Him. Some believers have more than one gift. I learned that my spiritual gift was faith. I also decided to serve in the media ministry at church.

What made me really enjoy media ministry was the out-of-the-box thinking Pastor West displayed each Sunday on the video screen. Pastor West would play a certain video as an illustration for his message and would eventually tie the video into his sermon. Each time I saw this, I was amazed because I did not know you could be creative when preaching God's Word. Pastor West taught me that you should never depart from God's Word when explaining the truth. However, you should think outside of the box to demonstrate and illustrate God's message in His Word. That is why I immediately got in the game and signed up for media ministry. Media helped the sermons come to life for me, and I wanted to be instrumental in helping others understand God's Word.

I was truly on my journey to labor for and to learn about Christ at the same time. My soul absorbed everything like a sponge, and my thoughts were constantly changing. There was so much more to learn, but I was on the right path.

8

THE GIFT OF FAITH

A Spiritual Gift Is Given to Me

There was something about the noun Faith. It's no surprise that my favorite singing artist is Faith Evans. However, there was something deeper that God wanted to teach me about this word *faith*. God wanted to make my faith become personal to me.

Before I got into the ministry at Sheepfold Church, I was encouraged to take a spiritual gift assessment online during our membership orientation. I had no idea what a spiritual gift was or how to take the assessment but I proceeded anyway.

After I took the assessment, I received a graph that rated my strongest spiritual gifts. Based on the graph, my strongest gift was faith. The second was evangelism. As much as I loved music, it was not rated as one of my gifts. I also learned that God gave me my spiritual gift through the Holy Spirit when I accepted Jesus Christ as my Lord and Savior.

The spiritual gift of faith is listed in 1 Corinthians 12:9. This gift simply means that I have an unusual reliance on God. I trust and believe that God specializes in the impossible. When things look impossible and all else fails, I believe that God can do the impossible. I believe that God is able! So when I feel limited and that there's no way out of something, my spiritual gift takes me to another level of belief. I know that God will show up even when I cannot see Him.

My faith tells me there is no dead end in God. God's resume (His Holy Scripture) paints so many examples of how there is no dead end in Him. Just when we think it's over, it's never over for God. Even in physical death, it's not over.

Therefore, it was no coincidence that the word *faith* stuck with me for so many years. I truly cherish the gift of faith God has given to me. It was part of His master plan for my life. I'm amazed that it first started with the name Faith, but who could have known God would eventually take me deeper into its meaning. Now I continually rejoice Hebrews 11:6 states, "And without faith it is impossible to please Him, for he who comes to God must believe that He is and that He is a rewarder of those who seek Him."

It is awesome to know that my faith pleases God. All I can say is, "Hallelujah!" He entrusted me with a gift and will use it for His glory. God is truly worthy to be praised!

9

A Pause for Reflection

I don't know what tomorrow holds but do know who holds tomorrow. As I take a moment to reflect on how far God has brought me, I realize I've been on a journey. I am forever amazed at what God has done for me in the past, is currently doing now, and what He has promised for my future. When I look back at my past, the question I continually ask myself is, *When has God ever failed me?* I keep getting the answer that He's never failed me. The same God who was there at the beginning of humankind is with me today on this race of a lifetime.

I feel in my bones that the Lord is up to something *big.* I don't know what the Lord is up to but He's planned something that will ultimately glorify Him. I keep seeking Him and pressing through with help from the Holy Spirit.

There's nothing like having a deep, intimate relationship with the Lord. Nothing! I'm going to keep moving forward through it all.

10

Back to Panama

2009

Happy Anniversary

Happy anniversary! Ericka and I were one year into our marriage. After many phone conversations and months of planning, Panama would be the place where we would spend our first wedding anniversary.

What better way to celebrate our one-year anniversary than to take Ericka to meet my mother, Laura, in Panama. I knew my mother would welcome Ericka with open arms. I simply could not wait for my wife and my mother to meet for the first time. They were the two most important ladies in my life.

To add more excitement to our trip, Nissa and my cousin Alfonzo (the same two people who introduced me to Ericka in 2006) would celebrate our one-year anniversary with us in Panama. My cousin and I had extended family in Panama. Alfonzo planned on visiting them while he was there. We also all planned to spend a few days on a resort in Panama City, Panama, before we would travel to Colón, Panama for the remainder of the trip to visit with family and friends.

I warned Ericka that life would be different outside of the resort when we ventured to Colón. The living conditions in Colón would be harsh compared to the resort. Ericka would eventually see why I was so grateful for all of the opportunities America had to offer. She would soon experience Panama for herself, but I would be right there with her in the process.

Panama City, Panama, Resort Pictures

In Colón, Panama

After leaving the beautiful resort in Panama City, we arrived in Colón, Panama, to be with family and friends. We first visited my Uncle Nesto's home so that everyone could meet my wife Ericka. His home was the central location where many family members would meet up.

After many months of planning, I was in Colón but could not make contact with my mother by telephone. I tried contacting her cell phone several times when I had originally arrived in Panama but I continued to get no response. Minute by minute, my anticipation grew because I could not wait for my mother and Ericka to meet for the first time, however, my mother was nowhere to be found. Inside my heart, I knew something was wrong. I continued to ask family members if they knew where she was but received only negative feedback.

My Uncle Nesto told me he had seen my mother late one night after he had gotten off work. He had asked my mother why she was out so late. She told him she was with a church group. The second thing my uncle told me was that he was worried about her because this was not her usual behavior. This was bad news, but I hoped it meant nothing.

I did not want my wife, Ericka, to hear about this, but there was no turning back. We were in Panama for a reason, and Ericka was now part of my family. She would have to witness some dark things in my family.

My mother finally arrived at my uncle's home. She came as if nothing was wrong and did not know we were trying to locate her. Either way, I was happy to see her, but something was different about her. She was not the Laura I knew. She had the same smile I could never forget, but I could also sense something was wrong. I did not want to claim this sense, but my mother was definitely up to something. I hoped and prayed she would not embarrass me in front of my new wife.

When Ericka met my mother, she could not see anything wrong with her, but I knew something was wrong. It was just a matter of time before something eventually came into the spotlight.

In Colón, Panama Part 2

When I had visited Colón, Panama in the past, I would spend my days catching up on family stories, eating, and trying to avoid the mosquitos. On this particular trip, Ericka and I, along with my cousin Alfonzo and his wife, Nissa, had other things planned for the next few days.

My cousin Alfonzo and his wife wanted to visit his father and extended family in Colón. This would be an interesting journey for Ericka and Nissa to see both of our extended families in Panama.

Before we could get started on our quest to see family, we had to establish a temporary living and sleeping place. Ericka and I had planned to stay at my Uncle Nesto's home, but the air was too hot and humid inside. He had no air conditioner in his home, and although I was used to this, it was not going to be a good place for Ericka to lay her head. It would have been torture for her. I could not put my wife through this agony after leaving the wonderfully air-conditioned resort, so we all planned to stay at a local hotel in downtown Colón. We would have an air conditioner and good sleeping arrangements. Most of all, Ericka would have peace of mind in a place that was very foreign to her.

In Panama City, Panama

Ericka, Nissa, Alfonzo, and I had a chance to hang out with family and to travel to Panama City, Panama for the day. We only had a few more days of our trip left to see as many family members as possible.

I learned that my paternal grandmother, Paula, had passed away prior to my return. This shocked me because the last time I had seen my grandmother, she had cooked me a meal. She hadn't seemed ill at the time, but my family said that when I had left Panama, she had become sick and had died. I was truly sad that she was gone.

As our time in Panama came to an end, again my mother, Laura, was nowhere to be found, so we could say our good-byes. Something was wrong with her, and Ericka was starting to feel my pain and frustration because I had been embarrassed and emotionally out of it during our stay in Colón.

I had expected our trip to be much different. With just one more day to go on our vacation and my mother missing, I gave up trying to see her before we all departed from Panama. I was very angry with my mother but deep inside hoped that she was okay.

As family drove us to our hotel, one final time, something strange happened. We saw my mother on the street walking with a man. I just looked at her as our car slowly drove by her. I was still angry with her, but Ericka did something bold. When the car came to a stop, Ericka quickly jumped out and approached my mom. She told my mom, "Your son is looking for you."

I quickly got out of the car and walked toward Ericka and my mom. The guy my mom had been walking with stepped to the side so I could have a conversation with her. I said, "Mom, where have you been?" I cannot remember what my mother said to me but saw she had white foam on the side of her mouth.

My mom was indeed on something. I told her we were getting ready to pack up and leave Panama, and I wanted to say goodbye to her. As we continued to speak, I told my mom that she looked bad. She repeated and said, "Michael, I look bad?" My mother then frowned and walked off.

It was a sad moment in my life because I was not sure if I would ever see my mom again, but I had to let her go. My mother was a grown woman and made her own choices. Our trip had come to an end.

11

SUBMERGED IN HIM

Baptism, October 4, 2009

He who has believed and has been baptized shall
be saved; but he who has disbelieved shall be
condemned. (Mark 16:16 NASB)

The more I learned about Christ, the more I wanted
to get closer to Him. I truly believed in what Christ
did for me on the cross, but there was something I
needed to do as I continued to grow in Him. To signify
what Christ had done for me by dying on the cross and
being buried and resurrected from the dead, I had to
be baptized. Being baptized is found primarily in the
book of Acts. When a person believed in Jesus Christ
and made a commitment to follow Him, this person
publically announced this inner commitment through
baptism.

One day, I rushed into Pastor West's office.
I desperately told him I needed to be baptized
immediately. I thought I would go to hell if I were not
baptized. At this time in my life, I did not even know
the true fundamentals of baptism or its importance but

wanted to be baptized if Jesus said it was important. I wanted to do whatever Jesus did.

On October 4, 2009, with all of my clothes on, I made a public confession to everyone at Sheepfold Church that I would belong to and follow Jesus Christ by being baptized in the name of the Father, the Son, and the Holy Spirit. It was another special moment in my walk with Christ.

Paul discusses baptism in Romans 6:3–4.

Or do you not know that all of us who have been baptized into Christ Jesus have been baptized into His death? Therefore, we have been buried with Him through baptism into death, in order that as Christ was raised from the dead through the glory of the Father, so too we might walk in newness of life. (Rom. 6:3–4 NASB)

When I was baptized, my actions told everyone there that I had a new direction and purpose for my life and that I trusted God to direct my life. My life would now be controlled and directed by the Spirit of God. I would have the courage and excitement to share Jesus Christ with others.

12

It Was Time To Meet Faith Evans

There's Just Something about Faith

It's no secret. I have been a big fan of the singer Faith Evans since I was sixteen years old. God has given Faith a heavenly voice, and I know it very well. Her music and her voice were a big part of my life growing up. In 2005, I briefly had a close encounter with Faith Evans and received four autographs from her in Minneapolis, Minnesota during her *First Lady* album tour. It was a powerful experience.

At that concert, I still remember a security guard telling me that I would not get an autograph from Faith Evans, but by the end of the night, I received the four autographs, which I mentioned earlier, without ever having a conversation with her. I would hold onto that moment forever but believed in my heart I would one day meet and have a conversation with her.

Let's fast-forward to the year 2010. I found out that Faith Evans would be performing in Houston, Texas, on October 29 (a Friday) at Arena Theatre. Now, I've never been to Houston. I know nothing about Arena Theatre but knew I was going to attend Faith Evan's concert. She was so close in distance and had taken a five-year hiatus, so I was going to watch her perform and promote her new album, *Something About Faith.*

Weeks later, Ericka and I sat in good seats at Arena Theatre. As always, I took in the moment. I had had a shirt printed with the word "Soon." This word came from Faith's video "Soon as I Get Home." Like any real fan, I simply wanted to stand out in the crowd. I had to let everyone know I was Faith's number one fan. As the concert started, the artist Slim from the group 112 was the opening act before Faith's performance. Slim put on a great show and got the crowd ready for Faith's grand entrance.

During the brief intermission and band changes on the stage, my heart started to pound quickly. I could not believe I was moments away from seeing Faith perform again. I was smiling from ear to ear. The stage was set and the lights in Arena Theatre transitioned to introduce the night's main event: Faith Evans. Before Faith came on stage, I heard the words, "Ladies and gentleman for your audio pleasure, the incomparable, the unsung one Faith Evans!"

This introduction came from the song, "Your Lover," from her 2010 album titled *Something About Faith.* My heart was beating by the minute as everyone in the theatre waited for her to enter the stage. I had my camera ready so I could take a close picture of her grand entrance.

As she came down the aisle, she spoke into the mic. I quickly ran to another seating section to get a closer photo of her. When Faith saw me, she pointed her finger at me as if to tell me she knew me. Could she have remembered me from Minneapolis in 2005? I didn't know. What I did know was that my wife, Ericka, witnessed her pointing at me before she got on stage.

Faith entering the stage

Me smiling from ear to ear wearing my "Soon" shirt

As she did in Minneapolis, Faith set the mood. Camera flashes were going off all over Arena Theatre. Faith, as usual, had that same spark she had had in Minneapolis five years earlier.

Faith talking to the crowd

As I waited, Faith got ready to sing my favorite song of all time, *"Soon As I Get Home."* She let the crowd know she was taking everyone back to 1995. The crowd went wild as she sang the beginning words, "Your Love … Is … Wonderful …" Her voice echoed throughout Arena Theatre. The red lights added warmth to the room as she began to sing. It was such a magical moment, and I took in everything through my memory and my camera.

"Don't Give Up Just Yet!"

As she did in Minneapolis, Minnesota, in 2005, Faith also put on a show in Houston, Texas, in 2010. She also sang a duet with artist Carl Thomas. The song was *"Can't Believe."* I knew the concert would be an experience I would never forget. I also knew I would have to drive four hours back to Dallas, Texas, and arrive by 7 AM when my shift at work started. I knew I would be physically tired the next day, but I was willing to make the sacrifice.

As the concert ended, Faith walked off the stage, and I tried to get a close-up of her. Faith saw me as she left the stage and posed for me. She gave me the green light to take a picture of her. However, I completely froze and didn't take the picture. I don't know what happened. I knew I had missed a golden opportunity to get a really good picture of my favorite artist. My time was up! Faith quickly walked off with her bodyguards. I stood there and was upset that I missed the photo opportunity.

I mean *she was right there!* Ericka witnessed the whole event as I continued to stand there in shock.

While everyone quickly exited the theater, I remembered hearing a security guard tell us that if we did not have VIP wristbands to go backstage and meet Faith, we had to exit the building. I wondered about the VIP wristbands. I hadn't known we could buy them to meet Faith in person. Wow! I had missed another opportunity, or so I thought.

A Dream Comes True

As Ericka and I were getting ready to exit Arena Theatre, I thought of something. I asked myself, *What if I could get backstage to meet Faith?* I know I didn't have a VIP wristband but did have four autographed album covers Faith had signed for me in Minneapolis, Minnesota, in 2005. I could not leave Arena Theatre just yet. Once we exited, there would be no turning back. I had to give seeing my favorite artist one more shot.

Ericka was on her way out of the door when I said, "Ericka, wait! Don't leave the building. I'm going to see if we can get backstage to meet Faith." My wife quickly turned around and followed my lead. I walked up to a security guard and told him I had traveled four hours from Dallas to see Faith and wanted to get two more autographs from her. I told him I did not have a VIP wristband. I did show him the four autographs from Faith I had received years ago.

I'm not sure if the security guard knew Faith's handwriting or not, but he told me I could wait in the line to go backstage and meet her. Just like that, Ericka and I were in a line with other fans waiting to see Faith up close. I could not believe I had simply asked and now was just moments away from meeting my favorite singer of all time.

While Ericka and I stood in line, I asked different people what their favorite Faith songs were and got a variety of feedback. It was interesting to hear how Faith Evans had touched each person's life. As we reached the front of the line, I could hear Faith's voice behind a nearby door as she talked to her fans and made jokes. Some fans sang for her and took pictures before they left.

When I finally got the chance to see Faith, I had the biggest smile and immediately said, "Hey, Faith!" Faith said she remembered my face but could not remember where she had seen me. I told her I was the guy she gave four autographs to after her performance in Minneapolis, Minnesota, in 2005. She quickly agreed with me.

Ericka and I sat next to Faith and grouped together with her to take a picture. Then I showed her the autographs she had signed for me in 2005 and asked her if I could have two more. These would be placed on the cover of her latest album and her Christmas album. She then asked Ericka if she wanted an autograph, but Ericka told her she didn't. My wife told Faith she was there to support me since she knew I was Faith's biggest fan. She said that I had bought a spray-painted shirt to support Faith. Ericka then pointed to the shirt I had worn to the concert that said, "Soon" on it.

After we took our picture with Faith, I was satisfied, but Faith told us that she wanted our information so she could keep in contact with us. I thought, *Say What? Yeah, right! Get outa here!* I thought Faith was joking, but she really wanted our information. Once again, I was in shock. However, I was not going to miss an opportunity to keep in touch with my favorite artist. One moment I hadn't thought I would meet Faith and now we were having fun with her backstage.

Faith was so cool and down to earth. She had a beautiful spirit like I had always imagined. I was truly amazed. I had first heard Faith Evans at the age of sixteen. I had wondered if I would ever meet her face to face. Now my dream had finally come true. It was a night I would never forget.

Backstage with Faith Evans

13

I ACCEPTED THE CALL

God Put Something Inside Me

Jesus says in Mark 2:17, "I did not come to call the righteous, but sinners." I took this verse of scripture as Jesus wanting to build the kingdom of God by using imperfect people such as myself to preach the Gospel. The more I continued to watch and to listen to several pastors, including Pastor West, preach the Gospel of Jesus Christ with confidence, clarity, accuracy, and boldness, something happened inside of me. However, I had a battle going on inside me. I wondered, *Is God calling me to preach the Gospel too?* Then I would think, *No way, God is calling me to preach the Gospel!* because I felt weak when it came to giving speeches in front of crowds. I knew that if God called me to do something, He had already equipped me for the task. But why had He chosen me?

For starters, I had so much to learn about God's Word. Secondly, I was afraid to stand up in front of crowds to speak. Thirdly, I was still as sinful as I could be. Yet something happened inside me every time I heard the Word of God preached. I truly loved the inspired Word of God. I believed that God's Word did work because my life and other lives change for the Gospel. I witnessed scriptures coming to life for me. But, why me? Again, something was happening inside of my heart, and as always, I could not battle with God anymore.

I accepted the call to preach His Word on August 15, 2011, at the approximate time of 8:12 PM. I accepted the call to preach His Word on August 15, 2011, at the approximate time of 8:12 PM. I remember I called Pastor West and told him of my decision to accept the call to preach God's Word. Pastor West quickly congratulated and encouraged me on my decision. I told Pastor West I was nervous because I did not know God's Word, and he told me he did not either. I was shocked that he would say this to me because every Sunday, I saw him teach from God's Word very clearly. If Pastor West said he did not know God's Word, I was in major trouble because he knew much more than I did.

In the midst of it all, God was doing something. I kept hearing the words, *Will you trust Me?* in my heart. God was asking me to trust Him completely with my spiritual growth, which meant complete reliance on Him.

As I would soon learn, preaching would create a long learning curve for me. I had so many things to learn. I simply had to trust the Lord for my development, and everything else on my journey would be part of the process.

14

MY FIRST SERMON AND
A SPECIAL GIFT

It was official. Pastor West finally gave me the okay to preach my first sermon on May 6, 2012. He did not give me a topic to preach on but wanted me to rely on the Lord for that. I prayed to God about what He wanted me to preach at Sheepfold Church, and He delivered.

The Lord led me to the story of David and Goliath. This story may seem elementary to many because everyone knows young David defeated Goliath in the end. Spiritually, God wanted me to see something that was much deeper, which would be beneficial for me while learning how to preach. This story was about training and the person God picks to do a specific task that will glorify Him. The David and Goliath story is full of many spiritual truths about courage, but most of all, how David had complete faith in the power of God to accomplish something major.

It wasn't a coincidence that the sermon God gave me would be on David and Goliath. I too needed to have complete faith in the power of God to give my first sermon. I needed to rely on God's power because I had a fear of speaking in front of people. This was the giant I had to face.

I thought it was ironic that the Lord led me to this story to learn some valuable tools. David was in preparation and would soon be revealed to Israel as a King. I too was going to be revealed to my church that I was man also called to preach the Gospel. David transitioned from a little shepherd boy in training to a hero who was noticed by all the people. I had come a long way in my life and was now going to preach God's Word. God showed the children of Israel that He could use a little shepherd boy to glorify Him. In the same way, God was using me, an imperfect person saved by amazing grace, to preach my first sermon about Him. Most of all, I was going to glorify God just like David did.

Consecrate Yourself: Pre-Sermon Preparation

On the day before my first sermon, I decided to stay at a local hotel to get away from all of the distractions of life and fully prepare myself to deliver God's Word. Pastor West wanted me to consecrate my mind. I didn't even know what *consecrate* meant but believed it had something to do with being focused.

I continued to remind myself to be like David and to rely solely on God. So all day and night, I studied, read, meditated, and prayed over my sermon. I really dug deep into 1 Samuel 17. Then I read it again and tried to hear from God. I read 1 Samuel 17 so much the story of David and Goliath became one with me. The Holy Spirit was helping me understand Scripture and allowing me to see David's preparation unfold right before my eyes. David's preparation never got old as I continually read about it. The message was timeless. I felt I was ready to go for the next day. I just had to pray about my delivery to the congregation.

The Pillar and Support of the Truth

In 1 Timothy 3:15, I learned that the church was the pillar and the support of the truth. This meant that the church supported God's Word and His truth. The church was the group of people who believed in and followed Jesus Christ. The church was me.

Now that I was a follower of Jesus Christ, I had to preach only God's truth in a world that stood against His standards. Moreover, I would also have to depend on Christ through the power of the Holy Spirit so I could live out the truth. While trying to live out God's truth, the Lord let me know I would encounter various trials, tribulations, and even my own personal setbacks. Just like the disciples who walked with and learned from Christ, I was on a path where I would continually learn from Christ. Just as the people in the book of Acts, I had to follow the same instructions given by Christ to continue to preach and teach the truth about Him.

It Was Time

It was time to preach and there was no turning back now. Before I got on stage in front of Sheepfold Church, Pastor West introduced me to the congregation. Many friends had come to support me. All eyes were on me as I finally took the stage with several pieces of paper in my hand, which were filled with notes and points for my sermon.

I started by telling everyone how far God had brought me in less than ten years. I shared of my move from Minnesota to Texas in 2006. I also explained how Ericka had been very instrumental in my life by simply sharing the Gospel of Jesus Christ with me. I told everyone in the audience that if I died, I wanted to thank Ericka for sharing the Gospel with me, which eventually led me to accept Christ for salvation through the power of the Holy Spirit.

As I stood there on stage, I tried to hold back my tears. I was truly thankful for Ericka. She had helped to change my life. It was through her obedience that I learned about Jesus and what He did for me on the cross. Now I am saved and able to testify and witness about the power of Jesus Christ.

I then prayed and asked God to speak to me and through me. I then asked some *big* example questions at the beginning of my sermon such as:

When teaching and preaching the Gospel, how do I tell others that everyone is not meant to be millionaire?

How do I tell others to love God with all they've got and to love people?

How do I tell others to repent and to be baptized in the name of Jesus Christ for the forgiveness of their sins?

I began my sermon with these big questions because they were also big issues in our world that stood against the standards of God. The truth is, we live in a corrupt world, and nobody can save a dying world except the Lord Jesus Christ.

As I preached, I tied my sermon to the story of David and Goliath. David too had to face a big issue when he faced the giant. I had to face big issues in the world when I shared the Gospel of Christ. David knew God was on his side, and I knew God was on my side when I shared the truth of the Gospel. The cool thing about David before he went up against Goliath was that he was being trained as he cared for sheep. I myself was being trained through the ups and downs of life. I realized I was always covered by the grace of God.

I called the title of my first sermon "Fighting by Faith Not by Sight," which stemmed from 2 Corinthians 5:7 where the apostle Paul says, "For we walk by faith, not by sight." I added a little twist to my title because I wanted to show David knew how to fight by faith and not by sight.

Because of his bold faith, David was not intimidated by Goliath. He knew beyond a shadow of a doubt that He could destroy Goliath because God had prepared him while he cared for his father's sheep. David testified that he killed both a lion and a bear because the Lord was on his side in 1 Samuel 17:36-37. When you're following Christ, it's a fight between good and evil, truth and lies, and flesh and the Spirit. Sharing the Gospel and the truths of God's Word involves a big battle all Christians face. We too need to know God is on our side in this good fight.

The apostle Paul said it best in 2 Timothy 4:7, "I have fought the good fight." Paul primarily fought the good fight when he shared the Gospel. He was not ashamed of and knew the Gospel was the power of God for salvation to everyone who believes (see Romans 1:16). Therefore, the fight is good according to the Word of God but is also a big challenge that the Lord is fully aware of. The same way David was sent to his challenge (see 1 Samuel 17:17–20) is the same way we are sent into the world to share and preach the Gospel.

Licensed to Preach the Gospel

After I gave my sermon, Pastor West came up and congratulated me in front of the congregation. I remember being concerned about my delivery. I kept asking myself, *How did I do?*

As Pastor West continued to stand with me, he surprised me by giving me a signed "Certificate of License" to preach the Gospel. Everyone immediately stood up and applauded me, but I honestly did not know the importance of the certificate. Later, I found out the certificate meant that anyone could invite me to preach the Gospel in his church.

Receiving this certification was a great milestone in my life. I continued to see God at work in my life. I knew it was just the beginning because I had so much more to learn. Oratorically, I knew I needed to work more. Then I was reminded of a famous Scripture in God's Word I had learned at an early age that said, "I can do all things through Christ Who strengthens me" (Philippians 4:13).

15

A Journey Home

A Road Trip to Gary, Indiana, 2012!

In 2012, I officially became a published author, and what better way to celebrate my accomplishment than to go back home to the city of Gary, Indiana, where the majority of my life had taken off at full speed. It was time for a road trip back home. I had to go back to where my running days had started as a seventh grader.

I had a list of things I wanted to do while I was in Gary. I wanted to promote my book *The Race of a Lifetime*. I wanted to see old friends, run a lap or two around Gleason Park, and run on Roosevelt High School's track, just to reminisce on my early days of competition. Of course, I would visit my old stomping grounds of West Side High. I also wanted to visit my old home on Connecticut Street in Glen Park because I heard the house had burned down years ago. I wanted to see the damage the fire had caused.

I simply could not wait to get home to Gary, Indiana, to catch up with everyone and everything. Gary was simply my home away from home.

Back Home in Gary, Indiana, 2012

When I finally arrived back to the "G," many memories flooded my mind. Although I had heard the city was declining economically, educationally, and spiritually, I still loved my city. The city of Gary had changed my life. I continued to pray for Gary knowing that God could turn the city around at any time.

The first visit on my agenda would be to Lew Wallace High School. A good friend of mine named Tiffany, who used to compete for the Lew Wallace track and field team, set up my first meet and greet session at the school. Tiffany also taught at Lew Wallace High School. She wanted me to share my book and to let her students know that I came from Gary and there was hope.

Before I spoke to the new generation of kids at Lew Wallace High, I was amazed as I walked through the halls of "The Dubb," remembering my eighth-grade-graduation ceremony in the spring of 1992. I had thought I would attend Lew Wallace High School after middle school. Now I know God had other plans for my life.

I looked at some of the pictures on the walls and remembered the familiar faces of many people I knew while growing up. Many were people who had competed with me in basketball or track and field. I also recalled competing with some of the runners on the Glen Park Ambassadors AAU summer track team in 1993.

Lew Wallace had a rich history of great runners. Who could forget the Lew Wallace girls' track team winning three state high school track and field titles in the 90s? It was incredible to be home in Gary and to recollect some of the best days in the city. When the Lew Wallace girls' had won those track titles, it had been a major event for the city of Gary. Of course, when I had been a kid, I hadn't fully understood the significance of winning state championships in Indiana, but they had been major accomplishments.

As I stood there reflecting on this rich history, I could not wait to share some encouraging words with the students. Some of these students had been babies or had not yet been born by the time I had finished high school in 1996. I would be talking to students between the ages of fourteen and sixteen. I had no clue what to expect with this next generation of students but would soon find out.

Encouraging Words

The time finally came to speak to the small group of students at Lew Wallace High. I openly joked with the group of students by telling them they had been babies when I had graduated from high school. I had probably known some of their parents.

The students listened as I spoke about how God had brought me so far in my life and how I had literally grown up several blocks away from Lew Wallace High. Then after my brief moment with the students, several of them wanted to take a picture with me or to ask questions. It was an honor and a privilege to talk to them and give them hope to move forward on their journey in life. I also encouraged the students to trust in God for their futures and to give life a shot. I tried to help them understand that there were other places outside of Gary, Indiana, they could explore.

It was a cool moment in my life to be able to share some of my life's personal testimonies and to be a blessing to others by simply giving words of encouragement. It was an honor to give back. Who knows, my words of encouragement could have inspired just one person. That one person could be the next person to help change a million other lives. You never know what God is up to! He always has a plan and everything will be aligned to His will.

A Journey to the Past

After visiting Lew Wallace High School, I decided to drive through my old neighborhood to see what things had changed over the years. I first drove to Bailly Middle School where my running career had started. I went to the gym and peaked inside. This was where I had first learned about cross-country running from Coach Young with his joker smile. When I had attended Bailly, the gym had seemed so huge to me back then. Now, the gym seemed very small.

Michael Layne

I was amazed at the artwork on the walls that brought life to the gym. The memories of my days at Bailly continued to run through my mind. To some, Bailly had been just a middle school, but for me, it had been a critical turning point in my development, which had started in the fall of 1990. My life had been forever changed at Bailly Middle School, and I would never forget it.

A Journey on Connecticut Street

Before I visited West Side and Roosevelt High, on the other side of town, I wanted to visit to my old home on Connecticut Street. I heard that the house had burned down a few years earlier, and I wanted to drive through and see the neighborhood for myself. As my mind continued to travel down memory lane, I remembered arriving in Gary, Indiana, in the summer of 1990. The neighborhood had been so vibrant then. Now I was going to compare those memories with how things were now.

When I arrived on Connecticut Street and saw my old home, a gloomy feeling came over me. The house was structurally sound and intact as I had always remembered it being, but all of the windows were now boarded up. On one side of the house, there used to be a nice open field where we played football and other sports, but now it was full of weeds and dead grass. The area had been abandoned. I walked the property just making observations, and more memories entered my mind. I thought about the days we had shoveled snow from and had played basketball on the long driveway and had thrown football passes in the open field.

Although it had been a dark moment in my life, I even remembered looking at the stairway, which had been attached to the house where my god-mother Marie had once stood and had told me not to ever come back. I had run away from home in the fall of 1992. In the present moment, things had changed after so many years, and it was sad to see my old home now in ruins. It looked lifeless, but my life had to continue on.

Gleason, Roosevelt, and West Side High

After my visit to Connecticut Street, I drove to Broadway Street to visit some more memorable places such as the gas station, which I remember quickly ending my prom night in the spring of 1996. It too was empty and lifeless.

I also drove by my Walgreens where I had had my first job at the age of sixteen. The store was now closed and empty.

I had to pause and reflect on how good God had been in my life and what He had done for me before I had a relationship with Him. Something about traveling back in time caused me to give thanks to the Lord for all He had allowed me to see. So many things had taken place in my young life, and I had no clue God had always been in the midst of them.

Next, I headed to South Gleason Park where my first days of cross-country competition had started. My life changed there by the smallest things. South Gleason Park had been the connecting point of just about everything. It had been my sanctuary. When things had happened all around Gary, South Gleason Park had been a place of solitude. I don't know how many laps I had run around South Gleason Park in my early years, but if it could talk, it would tell you I had spent a lot of my training days there.

Michael Layne

My next destination was Roosevelt High School, which was a little over a mile away from South Gleason Park. A lot of great races had taken place at Roosevelt High School, which we had called "Velt." During my era, Roosevelt High School would host both the boys' Northwest sectional and regional track meets before the state championships. Before you could make it to the state level in track, you had to pass both of these tough meets. If you did not make it in the top three spots per event at regionals, your high school track season was over.

I remembered that one of the many defining moments in my running career happened in the spring of 1993. I had stood on Roosevelt's track in front of the stadium timer. I could see that the parking lot was filled with cars and school buses and the stadium with fans. This memory sticks in my mind because it was one of the biggest races of my freshman year. I was very nervous, and my heart was beating fast at that moment. I had one shot to make it to the state championships, which was hard to accomplish in a Northwest regional meet as a freshman.

Michael Layne

Michael Layne

The competition was stiff, as I had to face many experienced runners from Portage, Valparaiso, Chesterton, and Merrillville, among others. Unfortunately, I did not make it out of the regional meet as a freshman but I remember the hunger within me after that race and the encouragement I received from my coaches and teammates. I looked forward to the future and wanted to get better. No matter what I had to face, running was going to be part of my life. The Lord allowed running to be my vehicle in life, which eventually took me to many destinations.

Back to "The Side"

There was no way I was going to travel all the way back to Gary, Indiana, and not visit "The Side," which is West Side High. I had never wanted to attend West Side High for school, but it had been where the Lord wanted me to be. Looking back, I am thankful how the Lord orchestrated my life. I now understand that His way is always best.

As I headed toward West Side, I couldn't wait to see the vivacious Coach Tiny and the everlasting Coach Johnson. These two amazing people also helped shape my life. I couldn't wait to see the hallways, the gymnasium, and most of all "The Surge" of West Side where so many memories had taken place.

When I finally arrived to "The Side," I drove on one of the largest parking lots in the world. I always felt West Side's parking lot was huge and very open. Everything was still the same as I approached the building, but when I finally entered it, something was different. Part of the building was divided into classrooms. I learned that West Side had students from seventh through twelfth grade. The school systems in Gary had gradually changed. The middle schools that had been located near West Side were no longer open. This had been one factor that had caused the change in grade levels at West Side.

As I continued to walk down the hallways I used to run and train in, the memories continued to enter my mind. I remember the freshman and sophomore halls had been located on the second floor, and the junior and senior halls had been on ground level. I knew where Coach Johnson's classroom was but still had to look for Coach Tiny's classroom. She was now teaching at West Side High since the middle school where she had been teaching had closed.

When I finally found Coach Tiny, she was the same woman I had known since the first day I had met her at age fourteen. In fact, she was more vibrant than ever. You could hear her energetic voice miles away. When we finally saw each other, we embraced and immediately started catching up on history and some of the craziest things from the past. Coach Tiny loved talking about her new roster of runners. Coaching was in her blood. In fact, coaching and being a surrogate mother to many of her student athletes was deeply rooted in her bones. She continued to show love and dedication to her students by teaching, coaching, and gradually changing each life, one at a time. She definitely played a major part in changing my life.

I visited my old training grounds on West Side's track

The major part of my visit was devoted to reflection time and catching up on life at West Side. I found Coach Johnson, Coach Tiny, and Coach Ronnie. These coaches along with Coach Benny and many other coaches were key people who helped shaped me.

While some things remained the same at West Side, I could see small changes especially in "The Surge." When I had attended West Side, there had been no benches to sit on in "The Surge." Now there were, which I thought was cool. There was a new roster of athletes with their photos on "The Surge's" walls, along with past pictures.

I felt honored my picture was still on "The Surge's" walls. I had been a part of the history at West Side, and it displayed our mascot Cougar pride. It was an amazing honor!

Michael Layne

"The Surge"

Final Stop: Trinity Baptist Church

I knew I had to pay Pastor Gardner a visit at Trinity Baptist Church. Pastor Gardner was very instrumental in changing my life and He also officiated my wedding ceremony. Pastor Gardner wanted me to visit his church to share words of encouragement as well as to promote my book.

I was nervous, as always, because I feared speaking in front of an audience. My mind would just go in different directions while I was looking at the many faces in the crowd and trying to speak. Some people have a speaker's gift, they speak loudly and clearly and stay on task in front of groups of people, but if I don't have my paper and notes with me, it is hard for to me speak in front of a large crowd.

Pastor Gardner introduced me and gave his congregation a brief history of our relationship—how we met and the story of my life. He then allowed me to stand at a side podium to introduce myself, to share some words of encouragement, and to talk about my book.

While I was talking, I saw some close friends in the audience who had come to support me while I was in town. I received solid support. In my brief speech, I remember telling the congregation that my wife Ericka could not be in attendance with me on this special trip to Gary because she was pregnant. I jokingly told the congregation I could not put Ericka through the torture of traveling sixteen hours by car with me. The audience quickly agreed with me.

After Pastor Gardner preached an awesome sermon, he told me to set up a side table in the church to sell my books. Pastor Gardner was so giving, He even told many of his members that if they did not have the money to purchase a book, he would buy a book for them. Many people then met me at the side table to share words of encouragement and to purchase my book.

I could not believe that just a few years ago before this I had told God I could not write a book. Now I was selling my own self-published copies. The spiritual lesson I learned from writing my book was if God had an assignment for you to do, He had already equipped you for the task. I had to be obedient and continually have faith that God knew what He was doing.

Pastor Gardner and me

16

A SEASON IS OVER

My Sheepfold Church Departure

For close to five years, Ericka and I served at a high level in Sheepfold Church under the direction and awesome leadership of Pastor West. Sheepfold Church taught the Bible. Our lives were changed forever because Pastor West taught the Bible in a clear way. My understanding of the Gospel continued to grow. There was no way I would ever turn back from believing in Jesus Christ because of the way Pastor West taught the Word of God.

Unfortunately, our season at Sheepfold Church came to an end because Ericka and I had to make changes. We were expecting a baby and could not continue to serve at such a high level of ministry, especially in a church that was located thirty minutes by car each way. There were many other factors but our main reason was its location. We were getting ready to become parents.

Before Ericka and I made the transition to leave our areas of ministry at Sheepfold Church, I prayed that the ministry work there would continue in a mighty way because the Word of God was being taught and lives were continually being changed. I did not want our absence to be a distraction while the church was trying to grow.

I also prayed that Ericka and I would find a church home that was closer to us and that believed in the same doctrine as Sheepfold Church. The truth about the Gospel of Jesus Christ was our foundation, and as the leader of my home, I had to make sure that our future church was on point with God's Word. Doctrine was very important to us, and we would not attend any place that deviated from the truth of God's Word. Eventually, God reminded us once again why He was God. He, as always, knew where we needed to be. Proverbs 16:9 says it well, "The mind of man plans his way, But the Lord directs his steps."

17

A CHILD IS BORN

A Gift from the Lord

On June 14, 2012, Ericka and I became the proud parents of a baby girl. We named her after both of her grandmothers. We were truly excited.

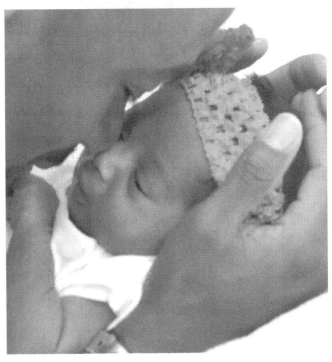

I don't know about Ericka, but again I witnessed the power of God on a different level when our baby girl was born. It was a journey that Ericka can really testify about on her time. One day when she is ready, she will allow me to explain our personal journey of becoming parents. I do know, God took us on a path where we would be able to see Him move in ways that blew our minds. Sometimes you go through a situation, see a miracle, and know it's the hands of God working right before your eyes. God did this for us.

Amazed is an understatement! Ericka and I were blessed with a beautiful and healthy baby girl whom God entrusted to us to be stewards over. Our daughter was a gift from Him. Our main job was to lead her right back to Him. Ericka and I carry this torch of stewardship with honor and our journey of parenthood continues.

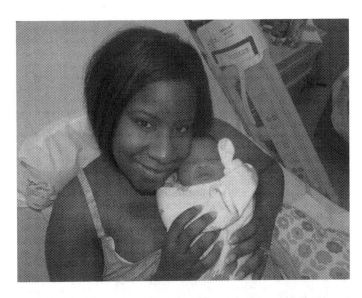

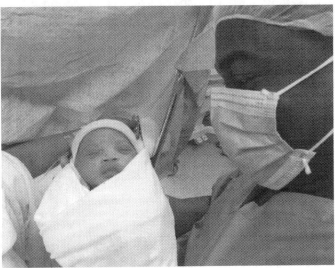

18

"WHERE IS YOUR FAITH?"

Tested

"Where is your faith?" In Luke 8:22–25, Jesus asked this famous question when the disciples were being tested in a boat during a storm. My faith was also tested on November 5, 2012. I had foot surgery in the prior month of October 2012. I had put this surgery off for many years. I needed the surgery because my running mechanics were getting worse as I grew older.

After the surgery, my left foot was swollen. After my body became used to the pain medication and the anesthesia had worn off, I was in excruciating pain. I was uncomfortable every second of every day. The pain seemed unbearable. As each day went by, my mind wondered if I would ever be able to jog again. Each day presented a different challenge for me mentally, physically, and spiritually. I was challenged so much on a spiritual level, I could not even open my Bible to pray and talk to God. I was suffering!

Things became worse in November. I woke up with more pain in my left foot. I immediately contacted my doctor to set up an appointment with him to see if something was wrong in the healing process because the pain continued to get worse by the minute. It was a pain I had never felt before. I knew something was wrong. The idea of my life being in jeopardy never crossed my mind, but something was brewing.

After my podiatrist saw the puffiness in my foot, he told me I had an infection. He prescribed some antibiotics and told me to get off my foot and relax. So I immediately got the antibiotics and took them with a meal. I waited for the medication to kick in, but the pain continued. I was hoping the medication would take away the pain, but the pain increased. Mentally, I kept telling myself, *I'm an athlete, and pain comes with the territory. I'll get through this,* but something was wrong.

By the late evening, I was on my knees crawling all over the house in agony. That's when I made up my mind to drive myself to the emergency room. I told Ericka to stay home and watch our baby while I drove myself to the emergency room. Before I knew it, I was on my way to the hospital and couldn't wait to get there. The pain continued.

When I finally made it to the emergency room, the receptionist gave me a clipboard with forms to fill out. I sat down, filled out the paperwork, and patiently waited for a doctor or nurse to call me. I then called Ericka and told her I had made it to the hospital safely. I waited in the lobby for about ten minutes until a doctor called me to come back. I told him I had had surgery on my left foot a month before and that it was in bad condition.

I was then taken to a room and put in a hospital bed. A nurse took one look at my foot and knew it was infected. She touched my foot and told me it was burning. When she finally took my temperature, she said I was running a fever.

Later a doctor came in the room and gave me some quick results. She told me she would have to keep me in the hospital because something was indeed wrong. Something was going on inside my body, and I had no clue what I was up against.

A **Close Call**

So I lay there in the hospital bed waiting to hear the results of my blood tests, which had been taken to determine what was wrong. Finally, a doctor came in and told me I had a staph infection that was traveling through my body. He said it was good that I had come to the hospital. He told me that if I'd fallen asleep with this infection, it would not have been good.

"Doctor, could I have died?" I asked. The doctor told me it would have not been good but never answered my question. I knew that people died from staph infections so I drew my own conclusion that this was what could have happened to me. I was shocked by this. Wow! Something inside me had kept telling me to go to the hospital. It had been the Holy Spirit guiding me to get help as I was potentially facing a life and death situation. The Lord was not done with me yet because there was more to learn.

Before I could grasp and understand this spiritual lesson, my faith had to be tested. I laid in the hospital bed not praying or reading my Word. I had my Word with me. However, I could not open it to focus on and be reminded of God's promises. It was easy for me to share my faith and encourage others but when my faith was tested in the storm, it was almost as if my faith failed. I didn't want to pray and talk to God during this trial. I was discouraged.

The Lord definitely knew where my faith was at that moment. However, He was not done shaping and growing me. I was still a work in progress. As I continued to lie there, I kept hearing, *Come to Me!* in my spirit. I could not open God's Word but continued to hear, *Come to Me!* over and over. The Lord wanted me to see something in His Word. Finally, I read Luke 8:22–25 where Jesus calmed the storm. The only question Jesus asked the disciples in this passage was, "Where is your faith?" This question continuously ran through my mind as the Spirit showed me that my faith would constantly be tested in the storm.

Just like the disciples, I had to be trained in the storm. So Jesus continued to ask me, *Where is your faith?* The more I heard this question, the more the Holy Spirit reminded me that Jesus was still in control of my life. Luke 8:23 said Jesus fell asleep during the storm, which showed me that He was present in the storm of my life but that He wasn't worried about it.

I pondered Jesus's question, *Where is your faith?* I became more and more encouraged to reach out to my

Savior. I had no control over the storm but was fully revived knowing that Jesus had complete control over it. He was right there with me and taught me as I continued to grow in Him.

19

FALLING SHORT IN GOD'S EYES

My Confession of Devotion

Simon, Simon behold, Satan has demanded permission to sift you like wheat; but I have prayed for you, that your faith may not fail; and you, when once you have turned again, strengthen your brothers. (Luke 22:31–32)

I love this passage of Scripture because Peter's faith was going to be tested. This was the training ground for Peter. Jesus knew the plans Satan had for Peter but also knew that Peter's faith had to be tested for spiritual growth.

Peter witnessed Jesus doing amazing things. Jesus granted Peter the authority to preach the Word of God, to heal the sick, to raise the dead, to cleanse lepers, and to cast out demons, yet he still denied knowing Christ three times. What I love about Jesus is He never turned His back on Peter. He prayed that Peter would not lose his faith after he failed.

I made this passage of scripture personal to me. Jesus has never turned His back on me even though I've failed Him over and over. What I have learned is that I must continue to press forward in my faith in Christ. I know and believe in what He did for me on the cross. He will gradually transform me to His image. It's a constant battle, but I know I'm on the right path. Christ has given me the privilege of getting to know Him and continually invites me into His presence. The closer I come to Him, the more my soul rests in Him.

The Lord is not done with me and encourages me the same way He did with Peter in Luke 22:32. He said, "When once you have turned again, strengthen your brothers." I'm amazed Jesus prayed that Peter would not lose his faith. Jesus knew Peter would deny Him and fail. Yet Jesus let Peter know that *when* he came back, he was to strengthen his brothers. This is astounding to me because Jesus didn't say *if* Peter comes back but *when*. Jesus knew Peter would come back.

After the resurrection of Jesus Christ, you see the amazing conversation that takes place between Peter and Jesus in John 21. Ultimately, Jesus forgives Peter, but on three separate occasions, Jesus asks Peter, "Do you love Me?" After each question, He commands Peter to tend to His lambs and shepherd His sheep. Peter would soon help change future lives because of the Gospel. Here we see the awesomeness of Christ. Jesus wanted Peter to recognize what He had done but He reminded Peter that He could still use him in spite of his failures. Peter had experienced forgiveness from Christ.

I felt this personally because even in my worst moments of disobedience and failure to God, He could still bring the best out of a bad situation. His Word says

Michael Layne

that He causes all things to work together for good for those who love Him and are called according to His purpose. In other words, I must have faith and keep moving forward because Jesus is not finished with me yet. He's still in control.

20

How the Trayvon Martin Tragedy Touched My Life

I am a runner for life. The Trayvon Martin tragedy touched my life in a special way because he could have been me. There were times I had wondered, *What if someone assumes that I am up to no good as I'm running in my neighborhood and takes my life? What if that person is not convicted but goes free?* The tragedy continued to weigh on my mind and heart.

I rarely ask God "Why?" I know He has everything under control, but this particular killing had remained with me for some reason. Again, I thought it simply could have been me, so I asked the Lord why Trayvon Martin was constantly on my mind and heart. God then took me on a journey.

Seeing the Trayvon Martin Tragedy through God's Eyes

I remember sitting in front of the television on July 13, 2013, and hearing the verdict that George Zimmerman was found not guilty for the killing of Trayvon Martin.

In my heart, I had thought he would not get away with killing a person but I was wrong.

I was upset because I continually imagined Trayvon Martin as being me. I asked myself, *Could I, a distance runner, be killed by a neighborhood watchman who assumes false things about me for reasons only God could uncover? Based on the false assumptions of a person, could my life be taken? Then to add more injury to death, could this person claims self-defense?*

I prayed for the Martin family because of this senseless loss. I leaned on the Lord to understand why this had happened and how a person could get away with it, especially with all the inaccuracies of the story. A life was gone. In a way, it was like the Emmett Till tragedy. I felt it was another approved killing of this generation and the world had to see it.

My mind continued to race as I heard the "Not guilty" verdict. The verdict came out on a Saturday night. I thought about the many pastors around the nation who had to preach sermons the next day while the trial remained on many hearts around the country. I wondered if any pastors would change their sermons and preach on the Trayvon Martin case.

If I were a pastor of a church, I wondered what my message would be, knowing many people were disturbed about the outcome. Would my message be about hurt and frustration or about peace, forgiveness, and complete trust in the Lord? As always, I took this to the Lord and asked how He would speak to me and through me if I had to preach that Sunday morning.

The Conversation between God and Me

God knew my heart was disturbed because I wanted Him to respond to this tragedy immediately. A life was gone, and someone had been set free from it. God questioned me as a believer in Jesus Christ. He said, *Why are you responding like a nonbeliever?* I pondered this question. God continued to remind me that He was still in control no matter how horrific things looked or seemed. He wanted me to put on my spiritual lenses and to dig deeper in His Word to gain peace and rest about the death of Trayvon Martin.

Jesus said it best in Matthew 28:11, "Come to me all who are weary and heavy-laden, and I will give you rest." I truly went to God and began to search His Word. This is what the Lord shared with me.

If everyone can recall, Trayvon Martin was killed in the darkness of the night on February 26, 2012. Some witnesses testified that they saw people struggling in the darkness. Some people heard cries for help. In my heart, I truly believe the voice many people heard on a 911 call screaming for help was Trayvon Martin.

The Lord wanted me to pay attention to the details that happened in the darkness. He asked me, *How is it that you live in a society where just about everything can now be easily recorded on camera by the click of a button, but no one could record the struggle of Trayvon Martin and George Zimmerman on camera in the darkness?* The Lord then asked, *If there were many break-ins in the neighborhood, wouldn't it be wise for concerned citizens, who were trying to protect their neighborhood, to petition for lights to be placed where there was darkness?*

As I sat there and contemplated these questions, I asked the Lord, *Where are You taking me?* The Holy Spirit led me to Psalm 139:7–12. This passage showed me that the Lord was omnipresent. The Lord wanted me to know He was right there in the midst of the darkness and chaos.

I then focused on Psalm 139:12, which says, "Even the darkness is not dark to You." The Lord told me He had seen everything but did not want anyone to see the true details of what had happened in the darkness that night. Therefore, no one could give a 100 percent accurate account of what had truly happened in the killing of Trayvon Martin.

At this point, I was still wrestling with the Lord. Then He challenged me to notice every time something terrible happened. The Lord said, *Michael, notice how many more people run to Me only when something bad happens. I, God, the Creator of all, immediately jump from being just an honorable mention to the top priority in many lives when chaos happens. I'm only recognized in desperation.*

The Lord showed me how man looked at fixing stand-your-ground laws or gun laws in America. The Lord asked, *Where am I in the midst of these law-fixing and decision-making discussions? Man only wants to fix things for man but takes his eyes off Me.* This is like the passage in Judges 17:6, which says, "Every man did what was right in his own eyes."

Then the Lord said,

Michael, remember the greatest crime committed against My Son. He suffered, bled, and died for humanity, and He was pure and innocent. He did nothing wrong! He was righteous! Where are the protests for My begotten Son Jesus all over the world as I commanded? He's the true and only Savior. His blood was poured out for the forgiveness of sins. This was a willful act to save all humanity. Where are the protests for salvation? I continue to say in My Word that no one knows the day or the hour his time on earth will be up. Many will perish and be without Me for all eternity because they did not believe in My Son, Jesus, for salvation.

Acts 4:12 says, "And there is salvation in no one else; for there is no other name under heaven that has been given among men by which we must be saved." Truly, those who believe in the birth, the death, and the resurrection of Jesus Christ are saved for eternity.

As I continued to talk to the Lord, I still asked, *Why?* Why would He allow Trayvon Martin to take a snack run to a local store and never make it back home alive? The Lord said, *I never promised Trayvon Martin that he would make it back home alive. As I continue to say in My Word, tomorrow is not promised to anyone.* I then pleaded with the Lord by saying, *He was young and minding his own business.* The Lord said, *Yes, I know this is sad, but this is why I want you to continue to tell young people that the Gospel is necessary in their lives. Every sinner needs the Savior. The world you live in gives false hope, but the only assurance for eternity is the belief in My Son, Jesus Christ.* The Lord continued, *Education, money, material things, and the temporary fixes of life that many people put their complete trust and hope in will not last. These things fade away but the Gospel will last and is important for everyone. It is dangerous to live in this world without the Gospel.*

Romans 6:23 says that the wages of sin is death. As I've learned, this is a three-way death. There is physical death. Everyone knows we all have to die physically someday. The second death is spiritual. If someone does not believe in Jesus Christ, who died on the cross for his sins, that person is spiritually dead to God. The third death, known as the second death in Revelations 20:14, is eternal death, which is complete separation from God forever. While people are still living and breathing, they have a chance to accept the Gospel before it's too late.

I then asked the Lord, *What was in George Zimmerman's mind and heart?* The Lord reiterated to me that He was the only One who could see both the mind and the heart of a man. He also wanted me to know that I should not be concerned with what was in Zimmerman's mind and heart. He asked me to simply pray for him. I quickly questioned the Lord again, *Pray for George Zimmerman?* In my flesh, I believed this man was a murderer who had used the law for his defense to get off free, but the Lord challenged me yet again.

The Lord told me to remember the apostle Paul in His Word. Paul was a man of the law. Paul used the law to persecute the Church. God said that in the same way He changed Paul and used him as an instrument, He could use George Zimmerman too. The question the Lord wanted me to ponder was, *If He decided to choose George Zimmerman as an instrument to glorify Him and to continue to spread the Gospel, would I receive the Word from him as a follower of Jesus Christ?* The Lord wanted me to see where my faith in Jesus Christ currently stood.

He also wanted to know if I could forgive in the midst of tragedy. John 3:16 tells us that God loved a rebellious world so much He gave His only begotten Son to save humanity. Our world did not deserve to be forgiven from sin. God wanted me to see the degree of His love and the immediate forgiveness He gives to a humanity that is undeserving.

Even though my flesh wanted to see immediate punishment for Zimmerman, I listened to the Holy Spirit within me and trusted the Lord. The Lord reminded me that He was still in control. I grew in peace each day that went by after the verdict. I could see things the way God wanted me to see them. My flesh totally disagreed, but the Holy Spirit within me guided me to refocus.

The Lord said, *Michael, My son, you have the Son because you believe in Him. In the wilderness of life, could you pray for, forgive, and most of all, love your enemy in spite of persecution?* God wanted me to see that this is how much He loved us. He loved a dying world so much He gave up His Son, Jesus Christ. Isaiah 53:10–11 says,

> But the Lord was pleased To crush Him, putting Him to grief; If He would render Himself as a guilt offering, He will see His offspring, He will prolong His days, and the good pleasure of the Lord will prosper in His hand. As a result of the anguish of His soul, He will see it and be satisfied; By His knowledge the Righteous One, My Servant, will justify the many, As He will bear their iniquities. (NASB)

21

A QUICK PAUSE

A Moment in His Word

Since I wrote this book, there have been numerous deaths and killings all over the world. If I simply marked the start date of February 26, 2012, as an example (the day Trayvon Martin was killed) until now, there have been many wars, mass shootings, homicides, kidnappings, terrorist attacks, hate crimes, and senseless killings. I am reminded what Jesus said Matthew 24: 6–14,

> You will be hearing of wars and rumors of wars. See that you are not frightened, for those things must take place, but that is not yet the end. For nation will rise against nation, and kingdom against kingdom, and in various places there will be famines and earthquakes. But all these things are merely the beginning of birth pangs. Then they will deliver you to tribulation, and will kill you, and you will be hated by all nations because of My name. At that time many will fall away and will betray one another and hate one another. Many false prophets will arise and will mislead many. Because lawlessness is increased, most people's love will grow cold. But the one who endures to the end, he

will be saved. This gospel of the kingdom shall be preached in the whole world as a testimony to all the nations, and then the end will come.

Two main things stand out to me in this passage. Jesus said, "Those things must take place," and, "But the one who endures to the end, he will be saved." In other words, those who believe in Jesus Christ are on the right path because these things were already written in the script from God. The great thing is that the Lord makes a promise when He says, "But the one who endures to the end, he will be saved." I call it pressing forward through the valley in the midst of continual chaos. It's one thing to say this but another to go through it. It takes the supernatural power of the Holy Spirit to guide and direct us in these tough times. Our flesh does not have the power or capacity to get us through these tough times. It is encouraging to know that everything God says is in His Word, so there is hope. I have a living hope through Jesus Christ and continue to press forward.

22

MAKING IT PERSONAL

"How Are Your Brothers and Sisters?"

"How Is Your Mom?"

Many people have read my book, *The Race of A Lifetime*, and have given me much needed feedback as I have continued to do the assignment the Lord has me on. After many people read the book, the questions that continued to come up in conversation were, "How are your brothers and sisters?" and "How is your mom?"

My mom is still alive and doing amazingly well. She is truly a survivor. You can see the hand of God on her life in an amazing way.

When it comes to answering questions about my siblings, it is difficult for me to answer. We all grew up separately. In our journeys, we were all going on different paths in life, and there was no togetherness between the six of us. In today's society, social media has played a big role in our lives because it has allowed us to communicate through cyberspace, but the oneness is still not there between us. There are a lot of unanswered questions. There is still pain, struggles, and unresolved issues. Most of all, a division remains between us all.

My mother, Laura, had six children: Michael (me), Odem, Telaya, Jaron, Ellis Junior, and Faye. Each of our lives was forever changed when our mother was deported back to Panama. When this separation took place, we all had to find our way. In my heart, I believe Ellis Junior and Faye suffered the most because they were babies when the separation from our mother occurred. They have no memories of our mother. They literally had to grow up and fend for themselves.

Through it all, I can still see God working in each of our lives. In the year 2000, I left the state of Iowa to move to Minnesota so that I could reunite with my younger siblings, Ellis Junior and Faye. I thought life would be better once I reconnected with them. I believed things would go back to how they were in the late 1980s. Because I was only twenty-two years old, I had no clue what I was up against. I simply had no plan at that age. The damage to Ellis Junior's and Faye's lives had already been done. I could not fix their lives. All I could do was try to understand their frustrations. Ellis Junior and Faye had many questions, and too many of them, I simply could not answer.

Odem, the second oldest sibling, battled a serious medical condition he still has today. Odem is a soldier. There are moments when I can easily see the grace of God on his life. I am a witness that God can make a way out of no way. He has done this for Odem time and time again.

Telaya, the third oldest sibling, is the rock for the rest of us. Telaya has been through so much in her life, but even today, she's still able to stand tall and testify about the greatness of God. She is rock solid and battlefield tested. One day, Telaya and I were able to talk on the phone for three long hours about her life and what she had endured in her teenage and adult years. Personally, I've asked Telaya to write her own story, which starts back from the time she and Jaron were abandoned in the country Panama in the 90s. While I was on my own personal journey as a student athlete at the University of Iowa, I had no clue what Telaya and Jaron were going through in a country where they had to learn Spanish to survive. Telaya's story could help many women in this world. One day I pray she will have the boldness to finally share her testimony with others.

Jaron, the fourth oldest sibling, does his best to try to fit into any possible situation. I call Jaron the crowd pleaser. When he too was abandoned in Panama and finally returned to the United States in the late 90s, he never attended high school. Jaron missed out on crucial parts of his young, developing life because he had not grown up in the United States. Jaron is a trying to catch up on the years he lost when he was abandoned in Panama but I too see the hand of God on his life in a mighty way.

For me, I am thankful that I am saved and now have a personal relationship with Jesus Christ. I know I'm being conformed to the image of Christ but I too have my struggles even today. I can testify I am a work in progress, but the Lord has always been with me through it all and won't let me go. I know He has a calling on my life as He does with my mom and siblings.

I truly believe if my brothers and sisters have the same one-on-one relationship with the Lord that I have, their lives will change and become clearer to them. I am a witness of what Christ can do when we allow Him to take control of our lives. I am a witness that the power of the Holy Spirit can heal us. The Lord is able to restore us as a family.

As a family, we must all teach the next generation our history and the love we have for Jesus Christ. I pray that one day we can all come together as a family no matter what trials we've endured. We must keep Christ as our true focus in our lives because He's the foundation that cannot be broken. He can hold all things together.

23

THE JOURNEY CONTINUES

I'm Still on Assignment and Not Turning Back

The Lord is still writing my story. I have more to do for Christ and I can't turn back now. I know I'm on the right path and my steps have been ordered by God. As I have been on the right path, I have learned from Acts 1:8 that I am here for a purpose and have the same power from the Holy Spirit to witness for Jesus Christ as the disciples did.

I've learned that the Holy Spirit convicted me of sin. The Holy Spirit also showed and helped me understand the truth of the Gospel. The Holy Spirit helped me accept the truth of the Gospel. My sins, past, present, and future, were forgiven immediately when I accepted Christ as my Lord and Savior. The end result is that the Holy Spirit gave me the gift of faith and sealed me as a child of God, never to be lost again.

Now that my eyes have been opened to this truth, I am able to look back on my life to see how far the Lord has brought me. Grace and mercy brought me to this point. Truthfully, I am curious to know where He's taking me, but my heart trusts in Him no matter what. In this race of life, the Holy Spirit forever dwells within me to guide and to transform me into the image of Christ. I am saved by grace through faith in Jesus, and although I will never be perfect on this earth, the Lord says I'm still valuable because He paid the one-time price for me and those who believe in Him. He encourages me to keep pressing forward with this message to others. And the journey to Him continues …

Acknowledgments

First and foremost, I want to give all honor, praise, and thanks to my Lord and Savior, Jesus Christ. I don't know the full plans You have for me, but I'm glad I'm in Your plans. May I continue to be the ambassador you ordained me to be.

To my wife and daughter, thank you for keeping me on my toes. Many days I struggle but then remember the Lord has put me in charge of the Layne household to lead you ladies back to Him. I will have to give an account to Him one day, so I'm praying He will say to me, "Well done my good and faithful servant!"

There are so many people to thank, starting with my family. In our family, there have been many moments of disagreement, hurt, and frustration, but I will always give you love and respect for contributing to my developing life. My family has been a major part of my development. I will never deny this! I love you all!

To the many pastors in Gary, Indiana, and Minnesota, Pastor Lane, Pastor Bean, Pastor Gardner, Pastor Turner, Pastor Ishman, Pastor Dilosa, and Pastor Scott, I know you were very influential in my growth in Christ. I want to say thank you for being great servants and for sharing the Gospel. To the pastors who are close to me in Texas, James Womack, Ken Bailey, Joel Soto, Maurice Pugh, Kareem Smith, Rodney Carter, and

Tony Evans thank you men for being lights for Christ. You have all made me really understand what it means to be an ambassador for Christ.

To pastors Paul Sheppard, Bryan Carter, Charles Stanley, I have never met you, but if I ever get a chance to, I will tell each of you how you've helped me develop a deeper relationship with Christ.

To William Branch (Ambassador), Trip Lee, Lecrae, Tedashii, and many more of you who share the Gospel through your music, thank you! Ambassador you were the first to open my eyes to your lyrics from the song, "Crumbs." Then my mind exploded from there to Trip Lee, to Lecrae, and to others. Thank you! May many more eyes be opened to God's Word because of the work He has placed in each of us and because of our Lord and Savior, Jesus Christ.

To my favorite artist, Faith Evans, it's been over twenty years and counting since I first heard your heavenly voice. Thank you! I'm glad I finally met you for the first time in October 2010. It was a dream that came true. You have been a great friend on top of having a hectic schedule. I still hear the words in your song "Again" that says, "But if I had to do it all again, I wouldn't take away the rain cause I know it made me who I am." We wouldn't take away any of it because it has made us who we are. It was God's grace and mercy that has kept us the entire time. I like the start of Philippians 1:6 that says, "He who began a good work in us," which means God has started something so He continues to work in us. So keep going, Faith! Thank you so much, and we love you!

To my extended family—not by blood but I still call you family—Sharon Peterson, Ethel Peterson, Catherine Sinclair, Coach Veronica "Tiny" Williams, Coach Benny Morgan, Coach Eugene Johnson, Coach Ronnie Bonds, Nancy Randolf, Momma Brown in Alexandria, Lousiana, Mrs. Diana my Neighbor, Terri Gaston and family, Don and Patricia Cormier, Sean Schuster, John Tazbur, Momma Christine Rogers, Aunt Carolyn Lane, my Iowa Hawkeye family, my frat brothers of Alpha Phi Alpha Fraternity, Inc., Thomas Carroll IV, Deke German, Gregory Bennett and the Bennett family, and my West Side Cougar family (so, so, so many people to name and to reach out to), thank you all. You have all played a major role in my life.

About the Author

Michael Layne saved by amazing grace and a follower of Jesus Christ. He is back again with his sequel, *The Race of a Lifetime: Second Wind*. He's still on a journey of growth in Christ.

It says in Romans 10:9 that once you've confessed with your mouth that Jesus is Lord and have believed in your heart that God raised Him from the dead, you are saved. It's amazing that once you're sealed as a child of God forever, it's not over. Jesus had to take his disciples on a journey of growth on so many levels, but most importantly, He had to grow them spiritually. Their journey was packed with many highs and lows, but at the end, there found a living hope in Jesus Christ. I'm on the same journey. My life is packed with highs and lows. However, I know I'm still on the right path. I'm being conformed to the image of Christ.

Printed in the United States
By Bookmasters